CHINESE MYSTICISM
AND MODERN PAINTING

CHINESE MYSTICISM

AND MODERN PAINTING

BY

GEORGES DUTHUIT

CHRONIQUES DU JOUR
PARIS

A. ZWEMMER
LONDON

The Chinese texts cited in the course of this essay have for the most part been borrowed from the following works : R. Petrucci, *La Philosophie de la Nature dans l'art d'Extrême Orient*, Paris, 1911; A. Waley, *An Introduction to the History of Chinese Painting*, London, 1923; O. Sirén, *A History of Early Chinese Painting, (The Medici Society)* London, 1933.

CHRONOLOGY OF CHIEF CHINESE DYNASTIES

SHANG	1766 B.C. to	1122	B.C.
CHOU	1122 ,, ,,	256	,,
CH'IN	255 ,, ,,	207	,,
HAN	206 ,, ,,	220	AD.
THE SIX DYNASTIES	220 AD. ,,	587	,,
NORTHERN WEI	386 ,, ,,	535	,,
SUI	581 ,, ,,	618	,,
T'ANG	618 ,, ,,	906	,,
THE FIVE DYNASTIES	907 ,, ,,	960	,,
SUNG	960 ,, ,,	1279	,,
YÜAN	1280 ,, ,,	1368	,,
MING	1368 ,, ,,	1644	,,
CH'ING	1644 ,, ,,	1912	,,

WHEN contemplating for the first time an exhibition of Chinese painting, the uninitiated visitor will not be overtaken by panic and trembling as in the days when Buddha spoke. Even if, on entering, he does not feel his heart to be peaceful, honest and sincere to the utmost, which is asking a good deal; even if he has not the reputation of a great and virtuous man; even if he does not belong— which is still more significant—to the rank of great officials; even if he has not mastered the Tao and knows nothing of the " spirit of the spirit which reveals the essence itself ", a perfect welcome is prepared for him. Dignitaries in white gloves will momentarily draw the curtain which hid from his eyes the depths of the abyss where the storm rages, where vaporous rocks tower aloft, where eagles brood in calm and repose. Sea monsters, marvellously tamed, will dance for his amusement in sinuous arabesques and he will perceive, on another roll, displayed with the same care, the Tartar cavalry arrested by silken lassoes, in the highest pitch of rapture, capering courteously and bending the knee for his honourable entertainment. One may feel intoxicated by sweetness before this flood of poetry which seems to flow in the distance; one will feel no shock of surprise.

The species of religious awe which formerly overwhelmed the student whenever he was confronted with Chinese painting was derived chiefly from his reading. The same phenomenon continues to occur to-day, although in attenuated forms. We are, indeed, constantly being offered essays whose sole aim, one might think, is to convince the reader of his unworthiness. How could we, mere Westerners, so earthy, so devoid of ascetism, understand pictures which draw their inspiration from speculations so transcendental, mystical and metaphysical ?

These European works are usually woven of quotations not easily accessible to the Chinese themselves, borrowed from authors of very unequal intellectual value and representing widely differing periods and societies. They thus present to us, in a most disconnected manner, a strange mixture of obscure sublimity and obvious *naïveté*. One might just as well fabricate, for the use of Eskimos, a treatise on European painting, starting with Plato and concluding with Berenson, going by way of Vasari, Winckelmann, Viollet-le-Duc and Marinetti. Such is the discouraging impression left by a first reading.

Not that all is disconcerting in these texts, even at first glance ; on the contrary. When they tell us that conformity with objects and fidelity to nature are conditions of good painting, we may disapprove, but we are not greatly disturbed. When again they inform us that colour must be applied according to each species, it may not seem very clearly explained, but we have no difficulty in agreeing. When they assure us finally that one ought to obtain solid construction, that plan and design, place and position serve to determine the composition, though we may not see the urgency of these remarks, we have no objection to make. We are at home. We advance with confidence. But where darkness sets in is when we learn, after having reviewed these secondary principles, that what matters first and foremost is the resonance of the spirit, the movement of life ; where we begin to fear is when we are invited to take the Road to Heaven, when we are asked to attain without

I

WU-CHUN, 1249. — CALLIGRAPHY.

Count Sakai Collec., Tōkyō.

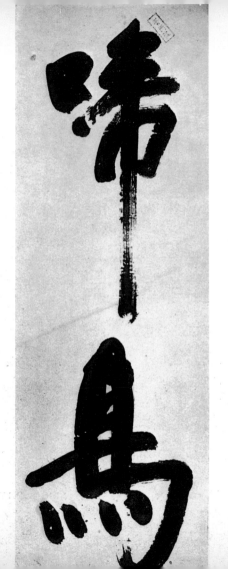

3

YING YÜ-CHIEN, Sung Dynasty. — VILLAGE IN THE MIST.

Count Matsudaira Collec., Tōkyō.   By courtesy of Dr. Sirén.

雨艇雪航歙長沙
後之殘虹常吸霞
最好市橋右柳升
酒旗招曳有烟家
　　山市晴嵐

4

Ch'ên Jung, 13th. cent. — Four Dragons by a Stream.

Boston Museum. *By courtesy of Dr. Sirén.*

effort the vital principle, quintessence of the truth, from which the truth proceeds; and that then, only then, shall we be able to appreciate the transparency of a bamboo thicket, the gracefulness of a garland of water-lilies deliciously paled by the wear of centuries...

If, according to the quaint advice of Tung Ch'i-ch'ang, one must have studied thousands of books before executing a painting, will it then be necessary, on the contrary, in order to appreciate this same painting, to forget the books which are written about it to-day? We would by no means recommend such a desperate course.

The critic, indeed, granted that he is interested in modern life,—we mean the life of the mind,—will consult these texts with advantage. They may be accepted in their confusion, if allowance be made for the rhetoric, whimsicality and sometimes humour, which their authors may have infused into them. We can at least extract a general tendency from these writings. If they often lead us very far from our classical culture, they bring us very near, on the other hand, to certain ways of seeing and thinking which belong specifically to our contemporaries in the West.

THE philosopher of our countries, shaped in the schools of Greece or Germany, looked at some pictures, statues or carvings and then proceeded to form hypotheses concerning the beauty, the truth, the higher life which the work of art enabled him to attain. It seems that in China not only the thinker, but also the painter goes the opposite way about it and assumes first, before judging or creating a work, the pre-eminence of the mind which allows this work to exist. Before he acts he must discover a twofold principle of elevation and conduct which will enable him to carry the undertaking to a successful end. From this principle, which the sages of the East do not appear capable of defining in words accessible to our understanding, the artist, nevertheless, derives lines of work, a sort of preparatory ritual and even methods of execution.

All that has been written, indeed, amounts to little more than this : what counts, above all, in the quality of the artist or his work is the "Resonance of the Spirit" or "Spirit Harmony". If that does not appear sufficiently clear, other translators suggest the term " Rhythmic Vitality ". Again, Okakura calls it the " Living Movement of the Spirit through the Rhythm of Things ". Are we drawing near to pantheism? At any rate we are going from complication to complication, unless we simply admit that there exists, for the painter, a spiritual power which communicates life and meaning to material forms, and that he must attain this power before taking part himself in the elaboration of forms. To gain access to the foot of the throne certain formalities are laid down, a certain disposition of heart and mind. It is, for the adept, a kind of royal, or rather divine, presentation ceremony.

We may now with less astonishment learn through the "Comments on Landscapes" (a work of which the first printed edition dates from the beginning of the Yüan period) that before taking up his brushes the painter must take off his clothes and sit crosslegged. That means that "he must nourish in his heart gentleness and cheerfulness; his ideas must be quiet and harmonious; the heart should be quiet, honest and sincere to the utmost, then the various aspects of man's gladness and sorrow and of every other thing, be it pointed, oblique, bent or inclined, will appear naturally in his mind and be spontaneously brought out on his brush."

The painter, then, voluntarily undergoes an initiation test. He seeks to discover the secret of the laws which seem to him to govern the forces of the universe. He has to climb high, to leave behind the running waters, the mountains, the clouds. He must soar above the *beau motif*, dominate the subject of his composition. By meditation he can discover the secret spring which plucks off the dead leaves, lets loose the avalanche, drives on the vagabond. Objects and living beings constitute no more than the instruments of a sacrifice, the accessories of an act of worship. It is not surprising, in these conditions, that the painter is jealous of his private life, that he requires a good studio in a suitable district, carefully lighted. Ku K'ai-chih, of the fourth century A.D., built himself a lofty edifice to work in. "He was truly," — says the author of the treatise, — "a wise man of ancient times." Indeed, "if one does not act in this way inspiration will soon be restrained, distracted, dulled or hindered; and how could one then represent in painting the appearances of things and emotions?"

There must be other possibilities, even in China. From these remarks let us merely retain the fact that the artist withdraws from the world, that he stands aside from its changing scenes, even after having much admired them, that he regards himself as an inventor. And Kuo Hsi, to whom we owe these notes, one of the celebrities of the Imperial Academy in the eleventh century, was in fact congratulated on his powers of invention. The old critics acknowledged with enthusiasm that his mountains were " coiled up like snakes, that his stones were heaped in forms like the devil's face, that the bare trees stretched their branches like the talons of some giant eagle towards the torn and tattered clouds... " We are entering fairyland, through the sphere of change, on the frontiers of the world of Chuang Tzü, the mystic poet, for whom contraries became identical. We see the first lights glimmering in the City of Illuminations. We begin to realise that the Chinese artist aspires to play the part of a clairvoyant.

Whether he succeeds or not, we find other things in his work than the report of a journey through a particular corner of the material and sentimental world, seen through a temperament, a tradition and a theory. The work to be done will be for him, at whatever point his effort may stop, a means of communion with the universe as a whole. He seeks to control the mass of the forces which rule the earth, the heavens and his own consciousness. Here we recognise certain points of Baudelairean aesthetics, as they are laid down notably in the sonnet of the *Correspondances*. The poet of perfected sensibility does not seek to translate an image or a definite circumstance, any more than a distinct

5

LI SUNG, Sung Dynasty. — ROUGH SEA.

M. B. Hayasaki Collec., Tōkyō. By courtesy of Dr. Sirén.

6

VAN GOGH. — THE CORNFIELD.

Photo Druet, Paris.

7

CHOU CHIH-MIEN, Ming Dynasty (*attributed to*)
FISH IN WATER.

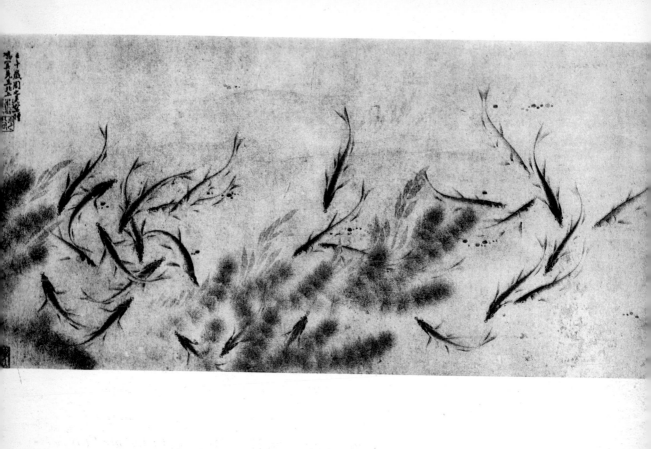

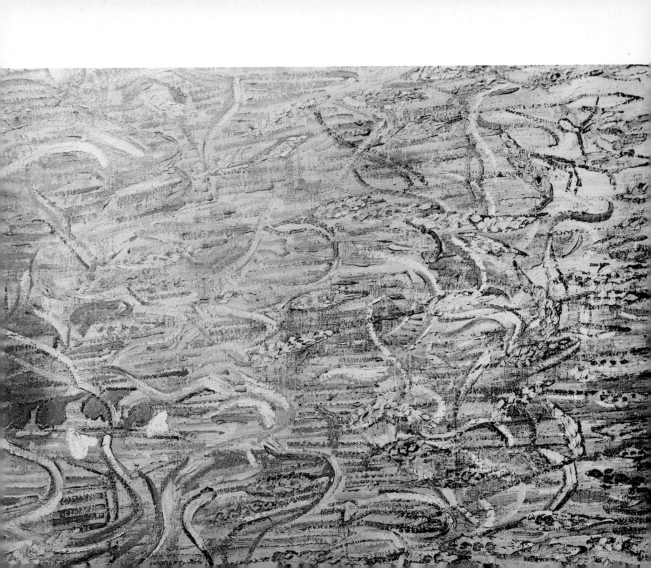

Van Gogh. — Submarine Landscape.

Private collec.. Amsterdam.   *Photo Bernheim Jeune.*

emotion. By his rhythms, his harmonies, his thoughts, he answers the voice of the hidden god, who through living columns murmurs confused words to him. Nature becomes for him a temple without limits, filled with loud or muffled echoes, where water is mingled with fire and clouds with stone. He must strive, then, to discern behind the walls the omnipresent reality of which human eyes, the reflections in canals, the smoke of factories, the dying sun, the radiance of female bodies form but the " dulled and plaintive mirrors ".

To us the mirror might well appear equally magnificent. Yet the important thing is to pass through the mirror.

This theory was adopted and for a time practised by Arthur Rimbaud with the ardour of a self-intoxicated adolescence, with all the impetuosity that an exaggerated verbal gift can give to a fiercely solitary nature. The rudderless ship was not long in running aground somewhere on the shores of the Red Sea. But skilful navigators salvaged the wreck. They pieced it together with much ingenuity, and set it afloat again after having equipped it with an exhibition hall, a circulating library and even a small printing shop.

Thus we had, a few years ago, dreaming courses, vision centres, a school where the director himself undertook to teach youthful pupils the best way to achieve, without too much trouble, derangement of the senses. The learners were not asked to " sit down before a bright window, at a clean table, burning a stick of incense to dispel all anxiety, in order that the fine verses and excellent concepts should take shape. " But the professors exalted the desire to work quickly, the necessity of soaring with a single beat of the wings as high as poetic intoxication permitted, then to come down with the sudden and terrific speed of an eagle to earth again, to make it our prey, our chattel, our mind's slave.

As there were to be found at that time certain members of the *Surréaliste* group as richly endowed with talent as with courage, they obtained results of considerable interest. In Europe their works did not fail to cause surprise among most of our contemporaries. There can be no doubt that they would in no way have baffled a cultured Chinese, that is to say a man whose forefathers were the first to track down and explore the fugitive lands of the imagination; not, indeed, in order to set up permanent branch offices there, but at least in order to send reports of their wealth while broadly noting down their outlines.

9

WALL PAINTING FROM TUN HUANG, 8th. cent.

Fogg Museum, Cambridge Mss.   By courtesy of Dr. Sirén.

12

DEGAS. — AFTER THE BATH.

Henri Lerolle Collec., Paris.   *Photo Druet, Paris.*

IT must not be thought that the moralists of the Far East were exclusively in favour of the advantages the artist derived from the aid of alcohol and drugs, of hysteria and suicide; far from this, they as often as not upheld the blessings of virtue. As a matter of fact, one is unable to find in their writings a coherent doctrine as to the best method to follow in order to achieve inspiration. The biographers record with much complacency that certain masters performed admirably when in a state of intoxication—which, to me personally, would seem a thing of extraordinary difficulty. About the year 1215, a Zen [1] priest, of whom we shall have more to say, called Mu-ch'i, came to Hangchow, where he rebuilt a ruined monastery. By rapid swirls of ink he attempted, with undeniable success, to capture the moments of exaltation and set down the fleeting visions which he obtained from the frenzy of wine, the stupor of tea, or the vacancy of inanition*. Ch'ên Jung, at about the same time, was noted for the simplicity of his life and the competence with which he fulfilled his duties as a magistrate. The vigour of his prose, of his poems and of the dragons whose rings he forged out of the foam of the torrents on an anvil of granite, was also praised**. Finally, he was admired for his habits of a confirmed drunkard. " He made clouds by splashing ink on his picture. For mists he spat out water. When wrought up by wine he uttered a great shout and, seizing his hat, used it as a brush, roughly smearing his drawing; after

---

[1]. "Zen": the Japanese name for the contemplative sect, which is more current in Europe than the Chinese form "Ch'an" (Sanskrit "Dhyāna").

* Pl. 19.   ** Pl. 4.   33

which he finished his work with a proper brush." One of the first painters of the sect, Wang Hsia, who lived in the early ninth century, would perform when he was drunk real *tours de force*, going so far as to plunge his head into a bucket of ink and then flop it over a piece of silk on which there appeared, as if by magic, lakes, trees, enchanted mountains. But none seems to have carried emancipation further, among these priests, than Ying Yü-chien, secretary of the famous temple Ching-tzü ssü, who would take a cat-like pleasure in spattering and lacerating the sheet*.

Many, then, are the ways which lead to grace. We might mention by the way that Tantric Buddhism was, in its most developed forms, distinguished by semi-erotic, semi-religious orgies associated with the cult of the "female emanations" of Buddha and by the cult of the gruesome. A reasonably well-informed modern author capable of staging these practices in an appropriate setting—say a mountain of hardened mud lost in a desolate steppe—would find nice material here for a *roman noir*, a rather forgotten form of literature which some are painfully attempting to bring back to favour to-day. This matter has but little bearing on painting, or even art. We allude to it only incidentally.

Since Imagination has been enthroned as sovereign, it must possess, in order to reign, some tested and dependable instruments slowly perfected by generations. It requires that the painter should place at its service a supple wrist, a steady and perfectly practised hand. The Chinese artists were primarily and perhaps above all calligraphers**.

* Pl. 3. ** Pl. 1.

Their historians continually repeat that painting and calligraphy have a common origin. Many paintings that we know, of the early period, while leaving quite a large place to the naturalistic content, seem to be built of one piece, in the manner of an ideograph. What they reveal to us above all is the character of a master, his suppleness, his firmness and the way he is able boldly to knit his figures into a single chain which returns on itself, and of which we see neither the beginning nor the end*. One learned to draw *motifs* as one learned to shape letters, generally by the study of the ancients. To study from masterpieces or from nature was all one.

The Chinese artist may attach great literary value to a picture, to the extent of apparently confusing painting with poetry when speaking of it. But when he paints, what matters is the concentration of thought and the prompt and vigorous response of the hand to the directing will. Tradition ordains him to see, or rather to feel as a whole the work to be executed, before embarking on anything. "If the ideas of a man are confused, he will become the slave of exterior conditions." And further on: " He who deliberates and moves his brush intent on making a picture, misses to a still greater extent the art of painting, while he who cogitates and moves his brush without any intention of making a picture reaches the art of painting." This seems like a kind of automatic writing. Draw bamboos for ten years, *become* a bamboo, then forget all about bamboos when you are drawing. In possession of an infallible technique, the individual places himself at the mercy of inspiration.

* Pl. 2.   35

Here and there a treatise tells in the minutest detail what the composition of a landscape should be. It gives the height of the mountains, settles the configuration of the ground, determines the character of the trees, the number of people present, the distance from the rock to the cloud, etc. Here the treatises go too far. But all these houses among the branches, these horse-shows, these patriarchs crossing bridges, these stampeding buffaloes, correspond merely to the stage properties of a travelling theatre. It is the duty of the virtuoso to make us forget his themes: we are there to hear the variations. It is the varying tone of the voice which affects us, the sustained power of its note, the command of the guide who draws us on without hesitation or fatigue, after having stretched his magic carpet over the abysses. Let the painter thoroughly master his vocabulary, let him then arrange as he will his lines, his tone values, his coloured surfaces. " When the hand becomes acquainted with the brush and the ink stone, it sometimes happens that it moves about as in play, without any attachment, trying to explore the hidden secrets, while the months and the years become long as eternity."

The Asiatic painter thus possesses a repertory of what are called " expressionistic" lines ; jagged strokes signify rage ; broad, sweeping curves have an air of contented motion. The repetition of a sinuous, flowing line suggests the gentle mood of the female figure, and so on. Van Gogh, after having discovered the Japanese, disciples of the masters to whom we owe these principles, uses the same expedients*. With him, a criss-cross of slanting lines will give the contour of a valley-side. Threads rolled up into balls, heaped up, create the pleasing

   * Pl. 5 - 8.

14

DEGAS. — TWO WOMEN, monotype.

Doucet Collection. *Photo Druet.*

16

ALBERT MARQUET. — QUAI DU LOUVRE.

Photo Druet, Paris

confusion of a garden. A carpet of bristles recalls the nakedness of the shorn countryside. A procession of zigzags carries the ploughed furrows of the plain to the horizon and spells the continuity of human effort. Cottage roofs, cypresses and stooks swept by the *mistral* are rendered by a succession of hooks, S-shapes and variously arranged spirals. Whirling rockets, a bouquet of fireworks, conjure up the fierce heat of summer. Van Gogh believed in the irresistible power of inspiration. We gather from one of his letters that he was likely to make a successful picture with all the strength and all the risks of improvisation, only after having failed in about a dozen.

In their highest creations the Chinese help us to forget the places we move about in every day : house, town or country filled with objects of measurable sizes and at measurable distances. They have none the less often made use of certain very obvious procedures to estimate the position of beings and things in space, that fictitious depth which we attribute to the world when we assume that it begins with one object and ends with another—the last *motif*, as is generally the case in the Sung landscapes, being perhaps a perfectly blank sky.

Our classical teaching implies that represented space can be contained in a kind of box whose front side has been removed. Aided by certain geometrically arranged lines of recession and by the process of tonal gradation, the elements of the composition are distributed to suggest distance within this imaginary receptacle. In many cases the Chinese painter proceeds in the same fashion. But, while remaining in the box, he manages most ingeniously to vary the points of view. On the lower part of the silk cloth or rice-paper you will see first, for instance, the bottom of a valley where the wood-cutter is wending his way; next a small hill is shown, in front of you, and above it a peak seen from a much higher level. Three different views have been taken by the same traveller, as if he were climbing a path cut in the wall of a cliff, lifting his eyes at each halt. He then fits together the three aspects of the panorama on a flat surface. Similar effects have been realised by the cinema camera, particularly when the operator takes his shots from an aeroplane in pursuit of fugitive objects, falling parachutes or other aeroplanes.

Jack Powell, the drumless drummer, pride of the London music halls, needs only two sticks in order to captivate his audience. With the ends of these he strikes the back or the legs of a chair, the floor-boards, the leaves of a palm; he beats the air and hammers his own teeth; he plays anywhere, on anything. The rhythms are linked up and contrasted with prodigious complexity. The sounds increase, diminish and blend with a subtlety so great that one can hear the spider spinning its web amidst the rumbling of the thunder. With only the whites of the eyes gleaming out of the blackness of his shiny face, with arms flung wide, the wizard stops at last before a breathless audience, as though appealing to the god of silence from whom he draws all these noises. Degas, in his way, juggles with a collection of mops of hair, vertebrae, shins, taut muscles; but it is movement that he is trying to capture. (The fresco painters of Tun Huang*, as early as the eighth century, did the same thing). In the course of the furious chase one can see him at rehearsals of the ballet taking up unexpected positions, circling round the

* Pl. 9, 10.

山含秋色近
燕渡夕陽遲

18

WU CHÊN, 1280-1354. — BOATING.

F. Abe. Sumiyoshi Collection.   *Photo Musée Guimet.*

19

Mu-c'hi, 13th. cent. — Monkeys on a pine tree.

Daitokuji, Kyōto.   Photo Musée Guimet.

model, jumping up to the ceiling, throwing himself flat on his face and twisting his neck up, thus with incredible speed multiplying the angles of vision. Even if the marksman manages to catch in its flight the arrow he has shot, his fingers, of course, can hold only an inert thing. But we recognise the vigour of his grasp, the perfection of the acrobatics and the way he leaps from object to object, reviving, as it were, the abbreviations of Oriental script, tightened and stretched to bursting point*. The tints above all, exquisitely selected, faultlessly adjusted, prepared in a dark room by the light of a gas lamp, among flower-beds of tulle and paper vegetation, bring us near to the colour of the T'ang masters, and are themselves able to unite, as might a ribbon winding hither and thither across the canvas, the figures which analysis at first had tragically isolated**.

The Asiatic favours the long sinuous line, the dress that trails from the swinging silk ladder. We ourselves, under other conditions and if only in Romanesque times, have used this mode of arabesque. We always feel spontaneously the power of the vigorous lash of a whip, impressive in itself and which, while rightly self-sufficient by its fulness and grace, nevertheless clings tightly to the reality of a thing or person, its appearance, character, and peculiar type. If the line is interrupted, to be resumed or broken off with marvellous purpose, the spectator, from wherever he may come, carries on the impetus and adds his contribution to the poetic atmosphere thus evoked. This manner of practising communion is common, it will be agreed, to the distinguished minds of all religions. Toulouse-Lautrec practised it with irresistible elegance, in the most disreputable places***.

The bloody tribunal of Abstractionism would accuse this descendant of the Crusaders, who willingly and hilariously, with mutilated limbs, delivered himself up to the dogs, of having accepted the compulsion of things with too much submission. His line is involved with the human types, these in turn stray into the subject, whence comes a stylisation in the Japanese manner which bears its date and soon goes out of fashion. The inquisitors of Purity would blame him for those police-inspectors' coats, brothel-keepers' masks, that insolent prostitution, that tarnishing of beauty, for everything which recalls the obscurity of the origins, the fatality of pleasure, the abject evidence of the end, for a kind of twisted moralism which has nothing to do with the true eloquence of the picture. Counsel for the defence would retort that in the first place these bitter annotations by no means lack eloquence and that in the second place they, personally, appreciate their historical interest. Lautrec, stubbornly leading the calvalcade of rotting poets, boxer-pianists, back-street beauties, ribald Erinnyes, smiling virgins tortured by the splits, through the mazes of a jungle of shoddy bazaar wares, in the midst of which one may nevertheless have glimpses of pretty butterflies and beautiful free animals — Lautrec will always remain for many the distant but trusty companion across the dangerous waters of adolescence. Quite apart from his extraordinary merits as a draughtsman, he makes himself loved as it were outside his painting. Such an answer would express the normal attitude of the man of to-day towards most of the painters of the Far East, who in spite of the esoteric doctrine which in some cases they claim to hold, usually retain a marked taste for story-telling. The monotony of the themes, however, the simplicity of the intrigues, the respectability of the actors make the play presented inside the Great Wall greatly inferior in picturesque appeal to the parades of the Moulin Rouge or of the Foire du Trône, as they were described by the corrupt but still superb descendant of the ancient sculptors of kings and wild beasts.

Hero of gangrene, stoic of nausea and last conqueror of his race, Count Henri-Marie-Raymond de Toulouse-Lautrec-Monfa, in the eyes of any inhabitants of the *Marais* must rank, for exotic colour, far above those Emperors who were teachers of handwriting, professors of watercolour painting, protectors of wits, presidents of Academies, lovers of wine, of recitations and perfumed ladies, and whose ability to forget the cares of government in favour of these lofty pursuits made Marco Polo wonder. The illustrated annals of the Sung, Yüan or Ming dynasties reveal nothing really unusual to us, which is all in their favour. They present to us admirably well-bred young ladies, a little precious, over-refined and careful of their attire; old men who seem to have no occupation except reading or strolling in the wilds, and who are invariably dubbed " sages " in the catalogues ; the splendidly clothed denizens of the sea, the forest or the aviary; the spacious scenery of water, snow or leafless branches. All this, except for the citrine complexions, could be found just as well on the banks of the Loire as beyond the Gobi Desert. In what respect is Nature in Chekiang more strange than in Auvergne? And we have our Alpine climbers, ecstatic citizens who go so far into the unknown that they are unable to transcribe what they have seen either with brush or pen!

Another optical amusement in which the Chinese willingly indulge consists in pushing apart the perspective lines which in our museums, by a now ancestral habit, meet on the horizon. The lines of recession become parallel lines, differently inclined in relation to the vertical and horizontal axes. Between these boundaries figures, huts, objects will all find their place, the nearest being put at the bottom, the farthest at the top, without any diminution of size. Nothing impedes the spectator's glance, nothing arrests his thought; he walks as far as he likes along the river bank, along the path cut in the snow. Without yielding altogether, Albert Marquet has been seduced by this manner, particularly favourable to flood effects*. Here again the aeroplane is very successful when it flies low over a country road or railway lines.

But in contradistinction to our artists, the Sung or Yüan landscape painter, instead of concentrating on the delineation of the objects themselves, is chiefly concerned to render the atmosphere which surrounds them**. It needs no more than the pin-prick of a boat on the smooth waters, the sharp crest of a peak surrounded by wavering glimmers, the open hook of a swallow's beak waiting for its food or the claw of a fern; it needs no more than a light smear of ink or a few touches of malachite green or lapis lazuli, for the immensity of space, or rather of the fluid element, to be suddenly grasped, provided with an appreciable quality and placed, with quick dab and unerring touch, within reach of our imagination. Our race scarcely possesses the faculty of thus raising itself above the pit, through the ocean of mists or with eyes fixed on the

* Pl. 15, 16.   ** Pl. 17, 18.

22

VUILLARD. — THE PARK.

Prince Antoine Bibesco Collec., Paris.

23

UNKNOWN ARTIST, Sung Dynasty. — BOATS.

Bahr Collection.   *Photo A. C. Cooper, London.*

24

WHISTLER. — NOCTURNE. Blue and Silver, Cremorne Lights.

National Gallery, London.   *Photo National Gallery.*

blue.   Chinese painting, then, just as much as Chinese poetry, has here brought a new shade of meaning into our culture, expressive of an experience familiar to us, but one which for lack of fine enough instruments we find it hard to translate : the second of eternity, indefinitely drawn out by dreaming, when we follow, it may be, the smoke of a cigarette whose consistency and fragility give a human measure to the vastness of a Mediterranean sky; or when we see, as falling night presses down its gentle strangling fingers, the fringe of a woman's scarf floating on a terrace, a quivering key to darkness and silence.

We had, nevertheless, at the dawn of this century, a poetic painting, a painting of states of mind, which was not without refinements of the palette.   Bonnard went to work with entangled wools, trails of smoke, sooty outlines.   By his side, Vuillard fitted together precious screens according to unexpected relationships, also proceeding by allusions and half tones, these sometimes relieved by an incisive note*.   The world, accepted in its confusion, only revealed a few familiar sights—the cat in its basket, the flowered wall-paper, the half-wound ball of worsted, the elbow of a woman reading, all united in the blurred and shifting background of feeling.   Here again, the Japanese had acted as intermediaries.   Their spiritual ancestors, the Chinese painters, did not shake off the dust of the world as much as their philosophers recommended.   They had even very cleverly exploited, thanks to the confusion of *genres* and with the help of a cunning blend of sounds, perfumes and colours, emotions which draw a great part of their keenness from memory : " Do you remember the evening when the north wind was blowing? All that is left you is the smell of rotten leaves, the discomfort of wet clothes, regret for the too brief summer and everywhere, everywhere solitude… " We have to treat it so heavily. We tread on ermine with boots of lead. These things should be written with a light finger, on the fog. They are said in three words. The Chinese " *au cœur limpide et fin, de qui l'extase pure est de peindre la fin,* " never wipes his eye. He never places his hand on his breast. He does not appear to believe in his misfortune. Above all, he keeps the distance, We are grateful to him for that. There lingers, nevertheless, about these lunar screens an emotional perfume, discreet but insistent. As for the emotion, we have soon seen every side of it. After a short time its poignant face, with blurred features, always unchanged, is in danger of becoming importunate. It is true that the Chinese, unlike our Western collectors, had the modesty not to hang their confidential outpourings on the drawing-room wall.

26

TURNER. — SNOW STORM AND STEAMBOAT.

Tate Gallery, London.   *Photo Tate Gallery.*

27

TURNER. — DURHAM CASTLE AND CATHEDRAL. Drawing.

Tate Gallery, London.   *Photo A. C. Cooper, London.*

28

MANET. — STILL-LIFE.

DRAWING too direct an inspiration from the same examples, Whistler attempted in the very same decade, with a limp brush and diluted oil, to set down the imponderable harmonies of the atmosphere*. This manner demands long experiments carried out in a field of vision with boundaries so remote that they become indistinct. It needs a draughtsmanship made supple to the point of concealing itself while at the same time remaining dominant. Through lack of these traditional and personal qualities the painter, at the moment when he wishes to capture the breath of the new-born day or the trembling mystery of night, is in danger of joining, in his fantastic enterprise, the German poet who dreamed of stuffing the moonbeams. With taste, wit and knowledge, Whistler got out of the difficulty as best he could. Hampered by his academic connections, Turner, tackling the same problem in the light of day, had already taken a singular decision. He had simply abolished drawing altogether. Nothing restrained his storms. Not a single branch was there to assuage their fury. The tempest overflowed in every direction. The Chinese would not have approved of this pulverisation of form. Three or four curves are brought off in a single stroke by Wang Wei, and there is a waterfall; but there is also, present and invisible, the rock that supports it and allows the liquid mass to unload itself**. Turner was however anxious to pay homage to light. With this aim he resorted, towards the end of his life, to a flimsy technique, to a fresh and transparent wash that connects him remotely with those who, in Sung times, sought the spirit which enfolds all things in the conflicts of flames and air, in the shifting play of mist and

* Pl. 23, 24.   ** Pl. 25, 26.

clearness. We recognise in his drawings one of their devices : to introduce large breaks between the lines of the foreground and background and then to emphasise these lines by varying their thickness in order to bring out the important places and essential colour-effects*. Cézanne often employs an almost identical method. He paints as it were in fish-scale touches, fully tinted on their outer edge, but rather discoloured towards the bottom, thus indicating the various distances without losing the lightness of the air in which his walls and foliage are bathed.

A chance resemblance this, although Cézanne had known and studied Edouard Manet, the lover of prints who strove with the weapon of the brush and the support of sometimes boldly contrasted colour, to bring about the reconciliation of fluid and solid**. If it occurs to us to turn our eyes from the Provençal countryside, trodden by the master with slow, almost hesitating steps, sensation by sensation, to the fantastic scenery of Honan, deftly pictured by an inspired Chinese, it is because of the fact that the tenacious French bourgeois, a revolutionary in spite of himself, plunges into the unknown after having meditated, as recommended by the wise men, upon construction — what they call the " bone " — and is able to extricate, with a single outline and a few hints of projections, the essential character and framework of a mass ; the weight of a colossus of stone and earth, for instance, its in-gathered impetus and ascending might. His native dignity also causes him to study the grave faces, the hieratic attitudes of human types firmly attached to their material environment; this is why we may, without undue fantasy

  * Pl. 27. ** Pl. 28.

and looking only at the decorative aspect, put a male figure, signed Chang Ssü-kung, side by side with a portrait of the lady of the *Jas de Bouffan*, immovable in a flower-pattern armchair*.

We find an even closer analogy between the lonely figure of Georges Seurat and the Master of Ceremonies Mi Fei; their methods of execution are fixed in advance and of such an impersonal nature as to be equally applicable, in almost any circumstances, in any locality and with any form of illumination, by the inventors, or (allowing for varying degrees of talent), by groups of disciples**.

The Frenchman's desire for a synthesis is doubtless more marked and of a higher and more complex kind than that of this Chinese. But the axioms of composition of these two artists were sufficiently similar for their work to resemble each other in general effect and frequently in their handling. Both indeed relied on the expressive power of colour to bring out the basic harmony of a series of related or contrasted tone values. Similarly both realised that colour intrinsically possesses certain definite qualities of sensuality, of solemnity, of gaiety or of mystery, and that these qualities produce in us emotions and sensations more rarefied than those aroused by chance effects of nature. It is not therefore surprising that the glow of a street lamp casting its rays on the pointed hat of a Parisian clown should shine as far as the region of Kiangsu where the Governor Mi Fei, critic, poet, calligrapher and eccentric dignitary, sat shading off his cones and domes with a care for cleanliness amounting, it is said, almost to a mania.

The Bracquemond collection of Japanese prints, formed in 1856,

* Pl. 29 - 34.　　**　Pl. 35, 36.　　79

initiated us into the art of the Far East; and since then the analogies between Oriental and Western art have become constantly more numerous, and been further increased by our growing knowledge of Islam and of primitive cultures. A " constant " of temperature has been formed, a new climate has developed here and to-day the most diverse temperaments evolve—in the best cases without knowing it—in the sphere of action of the ancient picture-makers of the Celestial Empire.

When Braque seeks to build up a caryatid in a thin and trembling line which hardly contains its volumes, or when Rouault scratches and smears the colour across the paper with his fingers, conjuring up his enraged judges and lawyers, their technique comes to them naturally across centuries and civilisations from the source of initial though there represented by Wu Tao-tzü or Shih K'o*. So it was with the Italians of the Quattrocento : the atmosphere in which they place themselves, despite their formal originality and their disparity of conviction, recalls to historians that of pagan Greece rediscovered through the unearthing of Roman marbles.

* Pl. 37-40.

3o

CÉZANNE. — ROCKS AT FONTAINEBLEAU.

Photo Druet, Paris.

31

UNKNOWN ARTIST, Ming Dynasty. — LANDSCAPE.

Bahr Collection.   *Photo A. C. Cooper, London.*

32

CÉZANNE. — LANDSCAPE, water-colour.

Photo Druet, Paris

AT the beginning of the T'ang period, the cultural streams of India and Central Asia, penetrating into China, deposited rich alluvium on the frescoes of Tun Huang. We have, belonging to the style of this period, landscapes which are no more than scaffoldings of turquoise, cinnabar and pearl white, of boldly transposed colours. About eleven centuries later, the Persian miniatures made their appearance in the Parisian studios. The little orchestras of the Iranian court, by the liveliness of their chords and the audacity of their dissonances, came to confirm certain artists in their recently acquired certainty that the real powers of a picture are found not in the interest aroused by the scene, the types and the event represented, but in the actual shock produced by the play of colours and the direction of the lines; line and colour, moreover, forming one. Gauguin then appears as an innovator*. Oscillating between the extremes of two traditions, that of the analytical West and that of the decorative East, borrowing from both antagonistic methods which he succeeds only painfully in reconciling, encumbered, moreover, with exotic themes and symbolical aims which often hamper his search, he nevertheless formulates a certain number of ideas which one will find prevalent about 1905 (the date of the first exhibition of the " Fauve " group, then led by Henri-Matisse and André Derain), but now clarified, polished and considerably widened.

Briefly put, the colours employed unmixed, susceptible of unlimited combinations, compose a spontaneously uttered language, able to be capable of being understood without any reading of the subject *per se*. Harmonies of tints and contrasts enable the artist to obtain a "luminous"

* Pl. 41 - 42.

painting without having to show lights and shadows. To render the same sensation the line was modified in its texture and proportions according to the dimensions of the canvas to be filled. At the risk of denying the truthfulness of appearances as they are recorded by the retina during our everyday existence; at the risk of sacrificing the accuracy of the measurements, they sought to discover, beneath the fleshly envelope, the internal structure of individuals and to bring out what in their character approached a general conception of life, a kind of religious conception peculiar to the artist.

Here again are certain of the tendencies of Chinese aesthetics adopted by our people with less subtlety perhaps but also with firmer conviction, a more clear-cut desire for liberation. For them the expression is no longer furnished by the features of the model posing, but it springs from the assemblage of painted surfaces, equally flatly laid down, the empty spaces having the same importance as the full ones. The figures are situated in a spiritual space to which we can set no limits, since the material world surrounds us on all sides at once, since our body is part of it, since its images are woven into the stuff of our consciousness. Here again there can be no question of measurements, or relationships, or scientific truth.

The Chinese follow the same route. They hug the coast, they feel their way along it with incredible skill but prefer not to put in at the port. Yet their paintings, if we hang them on the wall — where they were not designed to hang for ever — have a power of expansion which changes the quality of the atmosphere ; they mingle with the vibrations

SEURAT. — THE BEC DE HOC.

Kenneth Clark Collection.

of the daylight those of their quiet harmonies. Critics sought the reason for the excellence of the paintings of Yen Li-pên in the fact that they did not attach too much importance to outward likeness. We may assume that in T'ang art the figures and other accessories in a natural motif are little more than lifeless properties, which remain inert until the painter infuses his own blood into them. We would wish perhaps that this flood might flow less grudgingly. One almost regrets the perfection of a culture which forbids singing with a full voice. And also, in spite of the extreme discretion of the narrator, in spite of his prodigiously elliptic speech and his silences briming with allusions, there still remains in these spiritual productions a certain naturalistic residue which our modern schools might find cumbersome.

Thus, in order to give support to the central motif of a still-life, Henri-Matisse scatters around it numbers of four-petalled rose shapes, conventional flowers to which nobody could give a name*. Picasso goes further. After having placed a glass jar, a lemon, a bowl between hangings resembling iron bars pinched into the shape of pointed brackets, he distorts each of his objects in order to turn them into ovals with their ends drawn out into points, thus achieving the unity of his picture by the balance of more or less similar forms**. These things take place in the burning solitude of the intelligence! The negro wood-carvings too had passed his way.

We should recall in this connection that Professor Joseph Strzygowski, of the University of Vienna, sees a common origin in all the abstract arts, or rather in the systems of composition which are based

* Pl. 44.   ** Pl. 45.   99

on effects of colour and movement independently from description. This scholar locates the original spring somewhere in the cold regions of the North. The spirit of the North thus reigns everywhere from India to Mexico, from New Zealand to Siberia. On this assumption the *Rue de la Boëtie* becomes more nordic than the China of the Mongols. Chou Wên-chü, in order to give greater homogeneity to the elements of his composition, is content to scatter in an arbitrary manner tufts of quite recognisable rose-mallows round the sleepy child*. But if we consider the three ladies of Chou Fang listening to the music of one of their companions, standing against a neutral background scarcely broken by the hint of a tree or a rock, the total abolition of chiaroscuro and modelling, the devout intimacy of this scene of purified pleasure, its calm, due as much to the inflexion of the figures as to the intervals separating them, the manner in which they commune in the empty, illimitable background which contains them, all that would serve to describe a work like "*La Musique*" by Henri-Matisse, where the figures, constructed on a larger scale, with the aid of still freer and more simplified means, are gathered in front of an absolutely plain green curtain, in a single mood of delighted expectation and mutual enchantment**.

Do such works foreshadow that dynamic philosophy of art, the premises of which Western thought is so painfully attempting to lay down? The students of the East are striving to make us aware, so it seems to us, of the existence of a prime mover termed, for want of better expressions, " Vital principle ", or " Rhythmic Vitality ". This irresistible force ignores the distinct, the isolated and draws all things into the unity of its movement. Inaccessible to particular minds, the individual can still reach it provided he frees himself from himself.

In order to expound a somewhat kindred theory, M. Bergson would doubtless use the terms "pure creation", "Life" or "ceaseless outflow", equally loose when he applied them to æsthetic questions. Here the artist precedes the thinker. Some pictures of Henri-Matisse, in particular the portrait of a girl visualized within a studio on the Quai Saint Michel throws a strong light on these intuitions, and makes the words of the Taoist pregnant with meaning* :

" The anonymous mask binds together in one thought the various aspects of the sorrow and the satisfaction of men. The slanting body and the sheafs of curves which spring out of it form a balanced composition which depends on no external conditions ; the apparition becomes reality itself to the spectator. The whole expresses not the charm and the harmony of appearances, but that vision of a subjective and non-phenomenal life without which works of art are merely toys. A super-individual Will has intervened. The author has allowed it to do its work. Exploring the hidden secrets, allowing his hand to move as in play, giving up the idea of making a picture, he has ended by reaching the art of painting. His feet nevertheless remain firmly fixed to the ground. He speaks to us face to face. And the Parisian idol reveals the august presence which created her, without a precise destination, without any attachment to a religious community, in a perhaps more convincing manner than the paradisiac figures, rich and majestic as they are, traced on the walls of our old sanctuaries by the worshippers of Shakyamuni ".

WE have thought it best to avoid the word " abstraction ", so freely used by the critics of the younger school in connection with modern art and occasionally in connection with that of ancient Asia. *Abstrahere*, to draw away from... If it is a question of borrowing certain details from nature in order to set them down on a piece of paper in accordance with new relationships, there is nothing more abstract than a photograph. If, thanks to the proper manipulation of T-square and compasses, circles and rectangles appear on a panel arranged with taste, and if we admire these figures because, detached from worldly conditions and human convulsions, they constitute beauty in itself, there is nothing more abstract than the picture traced on the window pane by the frost. If, however, the personality of a creator, with its reserves of strength, of delicacy and of audacity, is thrown entirely his the line he draws on into canvas, we hold that this lineposesses the same reality as any production of nature, provided that the latter, in its turn, strives towards creation and penetrates into the future.

" Nature exists certainly, butso does my canvas " are the words of one of our contemporaries who cares little for verisimilitude. This seems to be what the group of Zen painters were out to prove, living in the hills of the Western Lake which sheltered their monasteries. There with the sole aim of discovering the Buddha watching in the heart of every creature, they devoted themselves to meditation, to mystic extravagances and at times to alcohol.

The doctrine of these bohemian recluses of the 13th. century is not easy to define. Some hold that Zen aimed at the annihilation of consciousness. If

37

Wu Tao-tzü, 8th. cent. (*rubbing after a design by*)
Kuan-yin.

Lin-Lao-Shan.   *By courtesy of Dr. Sirén.*

唐吳道子作

38

GEORGE BRAQUE. — FIGURE.

Photo Paul Rosenberg, Paris.

39

SHIH-K'O (?), 9th. cent. — A PATRIARCH.

Shohoji, Kyōto.   *Photo Musée Guimet.*

40

GEORGES ROUAULT. — MAGISTRATES.

so, it is not easy to realise the position of the artist at the moment of creation.   Successful experiments in this direction have, nevertheless, been performed by painters more or less attached to the *Surréaliste* group of the present day.   Others, on the contrary, see in the Zen doctrine a means of developing the creative faculties.   We are to awaken our pure, divine, inner vision ; to project ourselves outwards ; to establish contact with the universal spirit ; to become a part of the universal life. " To drink a drop of water is to drink the universal water "…. Perhaps we do this without knowing it, but if we neglect the Zen practices — both mental and physical — the priceless privilege of liberty and happiness will seldom be our lot !

Let us not be too regretful.   We also have our prophets.   They point, if not to the radiant countenance of Truth, at least to the neighbouring regions where her light shines.   " Verisimilitude has no longer any importance, for all is sacrificed by the artist to the truths, the necessities of a superior nature whose existence he assumes without discovering it." Thus spoke the high-priest Guillaume Apollinaire in the *Closerie des Lilas*. Thus would have spoken long ago, or very nearly thus, we may suppose, the Zen painter who, it may be remarked, met with the same hostility in official circles as the most gifted of our contemporaries do to-day.

Mu-ch'i had an immense influence in Japan as well as in China.   Were this intoxicated monk to return to life and to take part unwillingly in the so-called advanced movements he would no doubt encounter exactly the same resistance, apart from the few informed people, as that which he faced long ago with the indifference, one may well imagine, of the genius who is utterly careless of genius. " His conceptions were quite simple and natural; he used no ornamental elaboration but painted in a coarse and repellent fashion, not in accordance with the ancient rules and really not for refined enjoyment ". As courtesy is always triumphant in China, even the most exalted officials were able to recognise talent. This is why, when the painters of the Academy saw the " really mysterious works " of another inspired man, Liang K'ai, they could not help respecting him. And yet the commentator adds, becoming himself again : " But the paintings of this artist which have been preserved are all of a coarse kind ". Yet Chinese painting, with the Zen School—here showing a likeness to the present trend—was doing no more than carrying its initial tendencies to their extreme conclusion.

Prose may be used to describe a particular exterior or moral phenomenon. Painting, on the other hand, may be compared to poetry; it ceases to select, it aims to command the universe in its entirety. And words remain as necessity and habit have wrought them. They are less docile, less malleable than lines, values and colours. These materials may be employed apart from any descriptive purpose. " If the work of the artist ", says the Zen painter, " is not imbued with his vision of the subjective, non-phenomenal life, his productions will be mere toys. "

Although the adoration of nature in this way is part of a ritual cult placed in the service of the deities of the peaks and the river, consequently different from the mystico-pagan effusions of our romanticism, the dweller in the solitudes, in China, nevertheless experiences, in contact with the lofty places preserved from social corruption, protected

41

CHANG SÊNG-YU and YEN LI-PÊN, 7 th. cent. (*copy after*)
THE DRUNKEN TAOIST.

A. Stoclet Collec., Bruxelles.

42

PAUL GAUGUIN. — « I RARO TO OVIRI ».

Photo Bernheim Jeune.

43

Chou Wên-chü, T'ang Dynasty.
Child Mand Rose-allows.

Boston Museum.   *Photo Musée Guimet.*

44

HENRI-MATISSE. — STILL-LIFE.

Grenoble Museum.   *Photo Bernheim Jenne, Paris.*

from the industrial blight, a feeling in which passion occupies a great place, and comparable to love as much by the excess of its beatitude as by the violence of its aberrations. So much so that among the sacred poisons susceptible of stirring up the rich combustion of the intelligence, must be counted the ecstasies induced by the woods and mountains.

Like children who do not know how to calm the ardour of their blood, nor in what arms to throw themselves, and run for hours about the country, mingling incoherent phrases with their shouts, the God-stricken vagabond rushes across the fields of snow or stones, which scorch wonderfully his bare feet. He only asks of the icy streams and the roots just enough food to sustain his frenzy.

Domestic animals were venerated, for they have a place in the cosmic order, The horse, by its gait, re-enacts the regular movement of the stars ; it becomes a symbol of the heavens. The ox, patient under the yoke, represents tolerance, the earth's submission, But once he has left the " marble town " behind, the solitary devotee admires and shares the existence of the homeless and ungoverned creatures, whose vital impulse no bridle has ever checked. With leaps and gambols, the tiger and the leopard, the wild boar and the deer, bring to him their graceful or ferocious messages of complete liberation. The painter loves these untamed beasts because they seek the desolation of the plains and the wintry moors : " He must transfer to his brush the gallant splendour of their stride ; he must do that and no more ".

One has only to leave Paris to catch a glimpse of the heights. André Masson finds them by plunging his head into a tuft of grass ; he then gets up dazzled, with his ears still buzzing. The choir starts again under the guidance of another sun; the dragon-flies, the ruffled blades of grass, the ardent crickets*. The canvas is no more than an arena in which are marshalled the forces which preside over the slaughter, the love-making, the play, the escape. By his expert conducting, the battle is turned into a ballet, an accurately controlled dance of transparencies, of metallic gleams, of iridescent flames. At other times the painter dives to the bottom of an aquarium and brings up, fixed by his thought, like the veins and granulations in a block of crystal, the pattern made by fierce and cunning fishes, tracing and retracing their complicated filigrees among the whirlpools and sands.

A Chinese author of the 11th. century assures us that flying and walking, quickly or slowly, are superficial ideas. Such things he considers can be easily expressed. He holds, on the other hand, that ideas of leisure, severity and quietness, having a deeper character, are less easy to represent. Why this distinction? To discover, beneath the protective hide, the peculiar springs of a being, the essence of its personality, the intimate quality which provides it with a brief instant of independence and the part it plays in the concert of the world; to acknowledge that a grasshopper possesses a soul—perhaps even the soul of a king, a Buddhist would add—and to reveal to us its minute destiny, but one linked up on all sides with the joy of summer or the universal devastation, is this worth while any less than to render the enchantment of sleep or the drowsiness of noon?

After remarking that the apricots, hibiscus and plums of a painter

* Pl. 51-52.

were all in bloom at one and the same time irrespective of season, and that his men, horses and trees were " all out of shape ", the Chinese critic adds : " These works were not like those of to-day ". We still see paintings of to-morrow making their appearance. How should they be like those of the present? So we begin to find less vague the basic canon of Hsieh Ho, who states that the first thought should be for the brush-stroke, because it represents the beginning of Life. For André Masson also, the horse, the bird and the forest met on the way are ressurrected, on his return from the walk, in a single impulse. As the beasts and foliage have become mingled with the emotional rumination of the walker and with his inner drama, the skeleton of a leaf, a tuft of hair and a quivering feather suffice to make us feel the horror of the horse that swallows the bird. As in the Korean tombs, where tortoises and snakes are coupled and almost fused into one that they may crush one another the better, the line dominates everything and holds us by its intensity*. It teems, rends and devours itself, a vehement graph of the struggle and deliverance of a man, who, taking part in the tussle of the brutes, tears himself away and bends them to his will.

The critics of the Ming dynasty place Ni Tsan in the second rank of the " Four Great Landscape Painters " of the fourteenth century. But when this eminent personality declared that painting is nothing but careless extravagance of the brush, not aiming at any verisimilitude but only suited to the artist's diversion, his admirers did not seem to understand him. So much so that one day, while the painter was on a visit to the town, he was obliged to turn away a group of admirers who were greedily soliciting his works, but expected his compositions to be " something in particular, seen at a particular season ".   In the face of his interlocutors' discontent Ni Tsan merely remarked, modestly, that they might as well be angry with a eunuch for not letting his beard grow.   In this case it is likely that the visitors had forgotten to shave.   They clung insolently to their previous day's physiognomy.   They wished to remain where fate had put them, with their eyes and ideas sullied by habit. They did not know that Picasso was not only a Divine Painter, but a Wonderful Painter, since the Divine Painter, according to Ching Hao, author of a recondite essay on aesthetics, is he who makes no effort of his own initiative and whose hand spontaneously reproduces natural forms.

Now Picasso goes beyond natural forms.   He will happen on occasion, in a bout of brush-practice, to spirit a young lady into a skate, or change an amorous couple into a heap of entrails. He enjoys transforming a family of bathers, innocently engaged in the frolics of the beach, into a fantastic round of connecting-rods, sets of false teeth and genital organs.   In spite of these catastrophic events the tourist, with a little imagination recognizes his familiar companions of the Casino or the alcove, in a greatly shaken up condition.   But these are only preliminary exersises.   Abruptly the tamer's whip snatches the fabulous monsters out of the shadows, and if he did not add here and there the dot of an eye or the flick of a sphincter, one would think he was giving a body to the Chaos of legend, before the compassionate and blundering gods had provided it with those orifices which, intended to help it to live,

45

PABLO PICASSO. — STILL-LIFE.

Bell Collection.

46

TOULOUSE-LAUTREC. — THE CANCAN, drawing.

Photo Druet.

47

CHOU FANG, 8th.-9th. cent. (*copy after*)

PLAYING THE CHIN IN A GARDEN.

Ex-Coll. Lo Chen-yü, Tientsin. *By Courtesy of Dr. Sirén.*

48

HENRI-MATISSE. — MUSIC.

Museum of Western Art, Moscow.

Photo Bernheim Jeune, Paris.

only served to consummate its ruin*. It is in the course of these magic passes, when the monster and the whip are blended into one, when the bull disappears into the folds of the cape, when the painter returns to pure arabesque, that the true *aficionados* wake up. It is then that Joan Miró bestirs himself and comes to applaud the older man.

Joan Miró arrives, drawn along by a wooden locomotive and dangling on the end of a string a carefully drawn little sun**. The string waves gracefully in the wind. All around, the earth is bursting with pleasure and shooting out lumps of washing-blue, sulphur, coal and chalk which the traveller catches in their flight. He rubs them on a taut cloth and we have heat in the pure state. The balloon drifts away, the thread trails after it, grows longer, hovers and disappears in its turn. Nothing remains in the infinite blue but an imperceptible rift, as if the sky were about to open and whisper to us some rapturous secret. The affinities between Joan Miró and the Chinese mind are such that he even makes use of numbers in his canvases, which remind one of the effect obtained by distinguished connoisseurs of the Far East, who would add to the scroll of a master those poetical comments which not unfrequently encumber the whole composition.

These prodigies accomplished, the painter returns to his Barcelona studio. Sitting down before a bright window, at a clean table, his heart filled to the brim with peace, simplicity and sincerity, he waits for the varied aspects of the world to appear to him, and for the delicate images and excellent concepts to take shape. No one had ever before formulated these images and ideas. It is thus when you travel without looking back. The world, so exuberant and so destitute, with all its lulls and tumults, this world of deserts, cities and poles, is too big to be told of. We can at least say what it has done to our hearts, to our thoughts, in those privileged moments when we sum up our experiences in order to rise above them. There are perhaps not more things in our philosophy than in heaven and earth, but there is something different. With a blue square in which, with exquisite care, a black bar and a scarlet blob are juxtaposed the painter evokes the image of eternal winter, recreates the petals and dead twigs which through the ages have never ceased to bestrew the frozen mirror of all the ponds which the earth bears on its surface.

One would not dream of hanging a pond on a wall. The Chinese were not far from arriving at this simple conclusion. Yet, although they incorporated their calligraphy in their painting, they never made use, to our knowledge, of such an abbreviated shorthand as the present day schools whose tendencies they anticipated*. Their artists appear always to have meditated in front of Nature's scenes, even if they only retained an extremely simplified recollection of them. It was by observation of a monkey swinging from a tree that Mu-ch'i is able, with the aid of a grey and white ball, to produce the impression of accumulated energy, of springs waiting to be released. It was after having assured himself tangibly of the vitality, the resilience of a tendril that Jih-kuan outlined two claws which might belong equally to a crab as to a vine.

We are at a loss to understand the critics of old who regarded these dazzling fencers as clumsy craftsmen. We admire them, rather,

* Pl. 59 - 6o.

49

WALL-PAINTING, Between the Yüan and Ming Dynasties

A LOKAPĀLA.

British Museum. *Photo British Museum.*

50

HENRI-MATISSE. — PORTRAIT OF A GIRL.

Walter Arenberg Collec., Hollywood, U. S. A.

Photo Bernheim Jeune, Paris.

51

TOMB-PAINTING, 5th.-6th. cent.

WINGED DRAGON. Guken-ri. Korea.

Photo Musée Guimet, Paris.

52

ANDRÉ MASSON. — SUMMER FROLICS.

Photo Galerie Simon, Paris.

for their keenness of perception, their intelligent observation, the vivacity of their touch. There is moreover nothing in all this to tear us away from the earth, and modern historians exceed the bounds of enthusiasm when, taking up exactly the opposite attitude, they declare that these washes, mixed with the water of heaven, were laid on by the fingers of an angel. That is the doctrine, nebulous yet attractive, which has so far occupied our attention, even more than the works themselves.

THE Chinese masters, in spite of all the reserve of their aesthetic diplomacy, have but seldom reached an ideography so stripped to its bare essentials as to be in danger, among us, of becoming absolutely incommunicable. The same horror of vulgarity which now affects European painters, led them only to persist in that policy of reticence and subtlety which was bound to become discouraging in the end. Will they never consent to let us hear the resounding tone of a full orchestra, or give us the joy of a frank, outright explanation?

From the beginning, China appears to us as a sovereign so accomplished, so loaded with experience and grace, that it is difficult to see what succeeding times could add to its taste, knowledge and refinements. The bronzes of the Shang or Yin period emerge abruptly after the shadows of pre-history, in the second millennium B.C. and, despite the existence of the ogre-headed vessels, they already have the proud, discreet, self-assured bearing of a very old aristocracy and a delicacy as of hot-house blooms. Next we pass by the wart-covered bells, the pot-bellied tripods, the nebulous monsters of the sacred kitchen of the Chou. Then we recognise the austerity, the unadorned austerity, the intelligent realism of the Han epoch. Soon Buddhist preaching sends us saints with elongated bodies and evasive smiles, arranging their draperies about their long legs crossed at a sharp angle; they seem ready to reign, from the height of their indifference, over our cathedrals. Clothed by the successors of the best Greek dressmakers, heavy with the syrupy food of India, other apostles arrive, fat-cheeked, round-shouldered, telling, with a lotus flower in their fingers, of pacification and imperial majesty.

53

Tomb-painting, 5th.-6 th.cent.
Tortoise and Snake. Guken-ri. Korea.

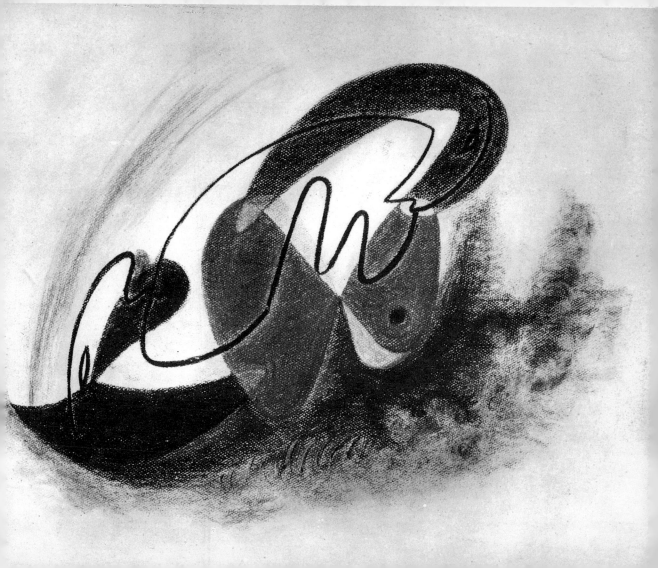

54

ANDRÉ MASSON. — HORSES.

55

Chang Hsü, 8th. cent. — Writing in the Ts'ao style.

From the Tu-t'ung t'ieh.

56

PABLO PICASSO. — COMPOSITION.

Photo Paul Rosenberg, Paris.

They are preceded by a whole procession of little bronze and gold figures, almost fainting from compassionate gentleness among bouquets of flames —fragile emanations of the Nirvana which is eventually to reclaim them.

Still later, we enter the orchard of the Sung, who nurtured their phials of congealed blood, their cups of frozen milk or translucent snow, their jars of evening fires or shadows. Their potters tender us, besides those bowls of black diamond which were used by the monks of T'ien Mu-shan, with exquisite manners, to offer each other tea, those dishes of a celadon so pure that it was believed to detect poisoned foods. And so we reach the reaction, the preciosity of the Ming dynasty which ended in the complicated and arbitrary techniques, the absurd falsification of materials of the Ch'ien-lung era. Now decadence reigns, that decadence which provided us with so many blood-curdling warriors, dogs bristling with spikes, over-elaborate lacquered cupboards and those fishes poisoned by their varnish, twisted in horrible convulsions around the colossal jars surmounted by pagoda-shaped lampshades with which our old uncle, a former ship's doctor, used to weigh down his piano. We have gone through thirty-five centuries of conquests, invasions, and fierce struggles for supremacy. We have met the witnesses of ancient sanguinary pageants, servants of hecatombs and mass burials, and those of periods of quiet concentration, fulfilment and dreaming. We have avoided the grimacing commercial travellers who represent nothing but a race thrown back on itself, exploiting its past from day to day, for the use of the " unclean swine " of the Western market.

And yet, when we have left the monumental effigies of religious inspiration, influenced by the people " from the West ", we cannot help recognizing in these things, in spite of the differencés of form, scenery and colour, a common origin, a similar destiny At the same time we do not succeed in understanding — for here again we become foreigners — why we have this same feeling about all of them. The paintings especially, in spite of the outlets of dreaming and the recreations of phantasy seem to us to exist only in a half-light, condemned to a perpetual quiet. They cannot free themselves completely; they are too near the administrative and mystic machine whose working must on no account be disturbed, put together once and for all by a genial watchmaker fanatically fond of precision, as if it were intended to revolve without a hitch for all eternity.

Princes have caused us to admire this precious mechanism.   We well knew that we had to hold our breath, to walk noiselessly in the rarefied atmosphere in which its works go round, and speak in a low voice; this attitude was not achieved without constraint.   Our delight in front of this restrained elegance and these muffled splendours was not enough to make us forget altogether that our hosts, voluptuous as they were, generally divided their cares between the cult of the tomb and the no less exacting one of a bureaucracy also ruled by the nobility of the dead. These mandarins without shadows or flesh, with their almost imperceptible outlines, standing here and there on half-opened scrolls, frequenters of the evanescent river-banks, the phantom forests and the dustless rooms, were of course mistaken when they called us " foreigners smelling of corpses ".   Ought they not rather to have reproached us for our evergreen health, our active passions, our despairs, our enthusiasms and our unimpaired taste for exalted life? Is it not purely because of our youth, our animal robustness, our future resources that we remained so foreign to them?

However it may be, we have come before them like respectful barbarians, grateful for the sumptuousness of the reception. We find in ourselves, too, numerous affinities with a race which séems always to have been led during its great periods by an infallible instinct to give Europe a lesson in popular distinction and high aristocratic bearing which we never needed so much as we do now. And thanks to the artists our civilisation, in spite of its failures and misunderstandings, remains one of the most open and comprehensive of all. So that one may see, now as in the ancient days, when Byzantium united Asia to France and to Romanesque Spain, our best workmen, cut off from their own countries, welcoming all the suggestions which seem good to them, whether they spring from their own being or have been for a moment offered them, from distant ages, by the Far East.

57

UNKNOWN ARTIST, Sung Dynasty. — AUTUMN MIST.

58

JOAN MIRÓ. — COMPOSITION.

59

JOAN MIRÓ. — THE LASSO.

René Gaffé, Collection.   *Photo Galerie Pierre, Paris.*

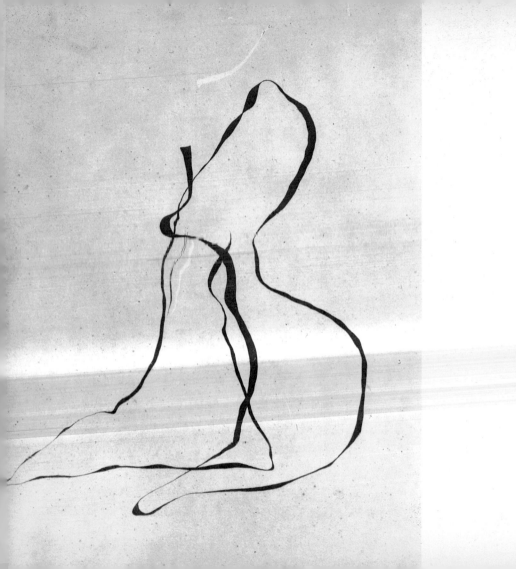

60

Jih-kuan, 13 th. cent. — Vine.

Tenryūji, Kyōto.   By courtesy of Dr. Sirén.

LIST OF PLATES

FRAZIER-SOYE

168, BOULEVARD DU MONTPARNASSE

PARIS